THE WOLVES OF YELLOWSTONE

A REWILDING STORY

CATHERINE BARR · JENNI DESMOND

BLOOMSBURY
CHILDREN'S BOOKS
NEW YORK LONDON OXFORD NEW DELHI SYDNEY

For Web with love, for wilderness adventures
still to come. —C.B.

For Grandma, who loves books, nature,
color, and noticing little things. —J. D.

BLOOMSBURY CHILDREN'S BOOKS
Bloomsbury Publishing Inc., part of Bloomsbury Publishing Plc
1385 Broadway, New York, NY 10018

BLOOMSBURY, BLOOMSBURY CHILDREN'S BOOKS, and the Diana logo
are trademarks of Bloomsbury Publishing Plc

First published in Great Britain as *Fourteen Wolves* in April 2021 by Bloomsbury Publishing Plc
Published in the United States of America in April 2022
by Bloomsbury Children's Books

Text copyright © 2021 by Catherine Barr
Illustrations copyright © 2021 by Jenni Desmond

Bloomsbury books may be purchased for business or promotional use. For information on bulk purchases
please contact Macmillan Corporate and Premium Sales Department at specialmarkets@macmillan.com

Library of Congress Cataloging-in-Publication Data
available upon request
ISBN 978-1-5476-0798-3 (hardcover) • ISBN 978-1-5476-0799-0 (e-book)
ISBN 978-1-5476-0800-3 (e-PDF)

Book design by Katie Knutton
Typeset in Jenni Desmond font
Printed and bound in China by Leo Paper Products, Heshan, Guangdong
10 9 8 7 6 5 4 3 2 1

To find out more about our authors and books visit www.bloomsbury.com and sign up for our newsletters.

With thanks to Leo Leckie, Yellowstone wolf historian and storyteller; Sian Jones, longtime
Yellowstone wolf watcher; the UK Wolf Conservation Trust, and Melanie Newton

THE WOLVES OF YELLOWSTONE NATIONAL PARK

The wolf is admired and feared in equal measure.

Shrouded in myth, this legendary predator has been shot, caught, and captured by humans for thousands of years.

Ranchers beware the glint of yellow eyes in the darkness, fearing a wolf has come to snatch their sleeping livestock, while trophy hunters seek out the wolf's thick, soft coat.

In fairy tales, the wolf's cry makes some shudder and others lock their doors.

But for many people, the wolf's haunting howl carries a wild magic—a magic that once restored a barren land.

A WILD AND BEAUTIFUL PLACE

In the United States of America, there is a park—a spectacular landscape sprawled across a sleeping volcano deep in the wilderness.

Spanning over 3,400 square miles, this immense park is found in the three states of Wyoming, Idaho, and Montana. On March 1, 1872, Yellowstone became the world's first national park. Today, around four million people from around the world visit it each year.

In the park there are rocks of every color, boiling hot lakes, and bubbling pools of mud. Snow-topped mountains reach toward the sky and, separated by wide valleys, there are dramatic canyons and rushing rivers. Hundreds of waterfalls gush down valley slopes. Here, some of the world's most famous geysers, natural hot fountains, shoot boiling water high into the air, while dark lakes reflect these surroundings like mirrors.

Yellowstone is home to nearly two thousand different kinds of wildlife. Over three hundred species of birds circle the sky above the park and nest in its thick forests. Colorful fish in all shapes and sizes swim through the streams. Proud elk and shaggy bison roam the wide plains. The park is the perfect hunting ground for large predators. Lynxes, mountain lions, black bears, grizzly bears, coyotes, and wolves all wander to seek out prey.

But Yellowstone hasn't always teemed with life. Once it was a place without wolves.

WITHOUT WOLVES

For hundreds of years wolves ruled Yellowstone. They roamed free and fierce over the wild plains, hunting the elk and other animals that lived in this wild land.

But as the years passed, hunters came and went. They snared the wolves for their warm fur and shot them if they chased or killed cattle. The U.S. government supported these hunters. They were determined to rid the wilderness of wolves, and park rangers shot the last wolf in Yellowstone in 1926.

The tracks of wolf packs that had claimed and crossed the park's remote valleys vanished. Yowling wolf pups that had once splashed through its rivers and streams disappeared.

Wolf howls no longer echoed across the land.

Without wolves, life in
the park changed . . .

Without wolves, the elk had
no fear. They grazed the open
valleys from sunrise to sunset.

Without wolves, the elk ate and
ate and ate. They ripped up grass
and tore down leaves. They nibbled
the young shoots that lined the
riverbanks, so fewer new trees
grew. The once lush grasslands
became barren and brown.

As more elk filled the wide valleys, other wildlife
began to disappear. Birds found they had fewer
places to nest, so many abandoned the park
for another home. Other animals lost their
shelter and couldn't find enough food.

But one cold winter's day in 1995,
wolves stepped back into Yellowstone.
The decision to reintroduce wolves
followed a twenty-year battle
between government officials, lawyers,
scientists, and conservationists.

This is the story of their homecoming.

7

· PART ONE ·

COMING HOME

SKY VIEW

This story begins in the sky.

High above the Canadian Rockies, a helicopter arcs above a line of wolves lunging through the snow. A man wearing a harness leans out, bracing himself against the bitter wind. He takes aim and fires. Then he unclips his harness and leaps out of the helicopter before it peels away.

The man has darted a wolf. It stumbles and falls ... and is soon asleep. Waiting hands on the ground help the man as he struggles to carry this beast across the snow. Together, they heave this soft, sleeping creature onto a waiting sled.

The sled dogs fidget, whimper, and stretch.
But when the driver steps up, the pack
lurches forward across the snow. The wolf
is carried away into inky darkness.

Another wolf is darted. Then another. And
another. This continues until fourteen wolves
are carried through the night on sleds
speeding toward a new home far away.

NIGHT
JOURNEY

The procession heads south.
The Canadian wolves crouch in
cold metal crates. In a small
plane they fly over rugged lands.

Soon they are hidden inside a truck and traveling
down a highway that cuts through some of the
wildest country in North America. The truck brakes
slowly. It pulls over. The crates are lifted onto
sleighs, this time pulled by mules with ice-crusted
manes. These hardy animals weave their way into
the heart of Yellowstone National Park.
In the distance, herds of elk gather in the darkness.

When the sleighs reach the specially built enclosures deep in the park, the crates are finally unlocked. A brave wolf steps out onto the white snow. His giant paws spread like snowshoes. He scans his new home with curious, intelligent eyes.

He is the first wolf to step into this wild place in a very long time.

WATCH AND WAIT

The wolves are kept in pens in three places in the park, each covering an acre of snow-blanketed land.

Although the wolves long to escape, they must stay in captivity for a little longer. If they are released too soon, the wolves' natural homing instinct will pull them north back toward Canada. In the pens, living is easy. People bring elk, deer, moose, or bison carcasses to the wolves so they can feed.

Behind the fences, the wolves bond and three packs begin to form, each one led by a dominant alpha male and female. This alpha pair is in charge; they are respected and feared by the other wolves in their pack.

The wolves wait for freedom. They pace the fences surrounding the pens. They learn new scents, sights, and sounds. They sense the wilderness beyond.

Ten weeks pass. At last, it is time for the wolves to run free.

ON THE RUN

The pens are flung open but the wolves
stand still. Scientists watch, holding
their breath.

They are not the only ones standing by. Many local ranchers and hunters are
angry that the wolves have been allowed to return, and so they linger in the
shadows ready to shoot and kill. Armed guards protected the wolves day and night in
the pens. But in the wild, the wolves will have to look out for themselves.

After three days the wary predators break free from their guards' watch and cross into
the wild. One by one, the wolves take slow, careful steps beyond the pens . . . quickening as
they vanish into the forest.

Now free, each pack establishes its own territory. Scientists name the packs after the
area of the park where they are released, calling them Crystal Creek Pack, Rose Creek
Pack, and Soda Butte Pack. Later, these three packs will become four, as a female from
Rose Creek and a male from Crystal Creek leave to begin life together as Leopold Pack.

Eventually all the wolves vanish from sight. But they are not lost. Each wolf has
been given a number and a radio collar, so it can be tracked. Signals from
the collars will help scientists map the wolves' travels: to discover
where they go and learn how they live.

Each pack journeys far and wide through dark forests,
across wild rivers, and up steep mountains.

The wolves of
Yellowstone are back
on the run.

ELK ENCOUNTER

During winter in Yellowstone, animals face a
relentless fight for survival. Temperatures plummet
as low as -30°F, rivers freeze, and a heavy blanket
of snow cloaks the earth. Food is scarce and
everyone is hungry.

Wolves need to eat and wolves eat elk . . .

When the wolves return, there are 19,000 elk on the move. In winter, the elk tread in each others' footsteps as they travel, saving energy to find food. They make their way toward the flat fields in the valleys where the snow is soft and the grass underneath is easier to graze. But there is not enough food to fill their bellies—the elk are weak and hungry.

The wolves, however, are strong. The elk are easy to spot in the open plains. The wolves watch them, waiting for the perfect moment to strike. They look for patches of deep snow, water, and ice, where elk may get stuck or fall.

The best time to hunt is when the sun is low and long shadows reach across the land. As the sun sinks, the elk stiffen, heads held high. Ears twitch, eyes widen, and males' antlers shift across the fading light. None of the herd has ever seen a wolf here, yet instinct still tells them that danger is coming. Frightened, they huddle closer together.

Black ravens watch as the wolves wait for sunset. And then the hunt is on.

17

THE HUNT

The wolves' powerful chests slice
through snow as they bound
nose-to-tail to save energy,
just like the elk.

The strongest wolves lead and the others follow.
Each wolf has a role.
They are a team.

A young elk has strayed to the edge of its herd.
The alpha female wolf spies the young elk, and
in that moment she selects it as prey. With her
signal, the pack begins to close in. The elk panics,
turning toward the safety of the river where
it thinks the wolves will not follow. It crashes
in through the jagged ice, legs scrabbling in the
freezing water.

The wolves wait for the cold to bite as the weak
elk finally, desperately, struggles back
to the water's edge.

The waiting wolves pounce. The elk is defeated. Exhausted from her effort, the alpha female sinks into the ground to catch her breath. Meanwhile, the rest of the pack tucks in. Everyone has earned this meal.

Ravens and magpies circle overhead and drop down, a delicate dance among feeding wolves. They will scavenge leftovers from the hunt. The predators have brought these birds their first meal in days.

The winter is fierce and long, but the winds of change are blowing. Spring is not far away...

THE BIG MELT

In March the big melt begins. Spring brings the sound of water rushing under ice.

As the ice slides away, these secret streams become churning, swirling cascades of water over land. They crash down the mountains to flood the valleys. Warmer temperatures bring wildflowers and green growth to the riverbanks.

Hibernating animals, such as black and grizzly bears, wake from long winter sleeps. Unlike wolves, these predators have been more protected in the park, and wolves will make their lives even easier. Hunting wolf packs leave plenty of leftovers— hungry bears seek and scrounge these wolf-killed carcasses across the park.

As the weather gets warmer, great herds of elk and bison fan out across the plains. With them come new calves.

GROWING UP

There are new arrivals in the wolf packs too.

Curled in the shelter of a den dug among the roots of a giant lodgepole pine, the alpha female nurses a litter of blind pups. They are the first wolves to be born in the Yellowstone area for a long time.

In a few weeks, the wolf pups peep out from their shady dens. They are curious and eager to explore their world.

The whole pack works together to raise the pups. They keep them warm and safe and help them learn how to hunt and fight. The young must pay attention—it will be a challenge to survive.

The lifespan of wild wolves can be short. If hunting is poor or if other predators snatch the pack's prey, then the pups will starve. As these little wolves grow, they learn to fight for territory and a mate. In years to come, many will die battling to be the leader of a pack. Others may be illegally shot by poachers if they venture beyond the park's boundaries.

But for now these pups are carefree. The knotted bundles of fur snuggle, feed, and sleep.

By midsummer, the wolf pups are about eight weeks old and strong enough to travel. Now it is time for the wolves to leave the comfort of their den and venture to a new home, where there is space for the pups to play and learn.

RIVER CROSSING

The wolf pack's journey brings new adventure.

Their destination is a flower meadow, where the grass is rich and plentiful.
But to get there, they must travel across perilous mountain streams.

The roaring torrent of water is ice cold, gushing from glaciers and snowfields
high in the peaks above. It's dangerous, but the alpha female knows that each
one of her pups will find the courage to take the plunge. Stepping cautiously into
cold water, she leads the way. She allows herself to be pulled downstream by the
dragging current, and she hauls herself onto a wide bank where she will wait.

One by one the pups step into the water, whimpering with the cold. The water is powerful and sweeps their little bodies downstream, but the female is ready to catch them before they drift too far. She pulls each pup out as it tumbles past.

Safely across, the pups stand on wobbly legs, shaking rainbows of water droplets on the opposite bank. Soon they are dry and ready to play in the summer sun.

SUMMER OF WOLVES

After a long journey, the wolves find
a meadow. The adults doze in the
summer heat, while the pups play
in the long grass.

When dusk falls, the adults
must shake off their sleep and
prepare to hunt. Eventually, the growing
pups will join the adults at the kill,
watching and learning. But for now
they must stay behind.

The wolves bring back an elk feast that
will provide food not only for the pack and
its hungry young, but for many other
animals watching and waiting for
scraps and bones.

And so it continues as the years pass.

Each spring, new litters of pups are born. As the number of wolves in the park increases, existing wolf packs change and new packs are formed.

The wolves are at the top of the food chain again.

With the return of the wolves, life for all the animals in the park changes and the landscape begins to shift in remarkable ways.

· PART TWO ·

A NEW YELLOWSTONE

RISE OF THE WOLVES

THE BALANCE OF NATURE BEGINS TO SHIFT . . .

The wolves are hungry and wolves eat elk.
The once enormous herds begin to shrink.

Now in competition with wolves
who will kill them, the number
of coyotes begins to fall.

With fewer coyotes to eat them, the
numbers of other animals rise.

Herds of pronghorn antelope grow.

More badgers scurry.

Families of foxes multiply.

The number of smaller mammals, such as timid
rabbits and mice, in the park is greater too.

WILLOW

COTTONWOOD TREE

SONGBIRDS FLOURISH

As the trees grow, their canopies of overhanging branches create shade and cool the river, making perfect places for birds to nest and rest.

The songbirds flourish. Warblers, flycatchers, gray catbirds, and mountain bluebirds perch and hop above the rivers below.

More migrating birds seek refuge in the park. Ospreys return from their winter flight, peregrine falcons soar through the sky, and white pelicans gulp down fish from the lakes and rivers.

FLYCATCHER

MOUNTAIN BLUEBIRD

OSPREY

GRAY
CATBIRD

WARBLER

PEREGRINE
FALCON

WHITE
PELICAN

33

BUILDING DAMS AND MAKING POOLS

The flood plains grow lush with the different plants, strengthening the banks of the river and creating new watery habitats.

BEAVER DAM

DUCKS

RAISED WATER

FROGS AND TOADS

FOOD STORE

AMPHIBIANS

SALAMANDERS

SNAILS

BEAVERS

INSECTS

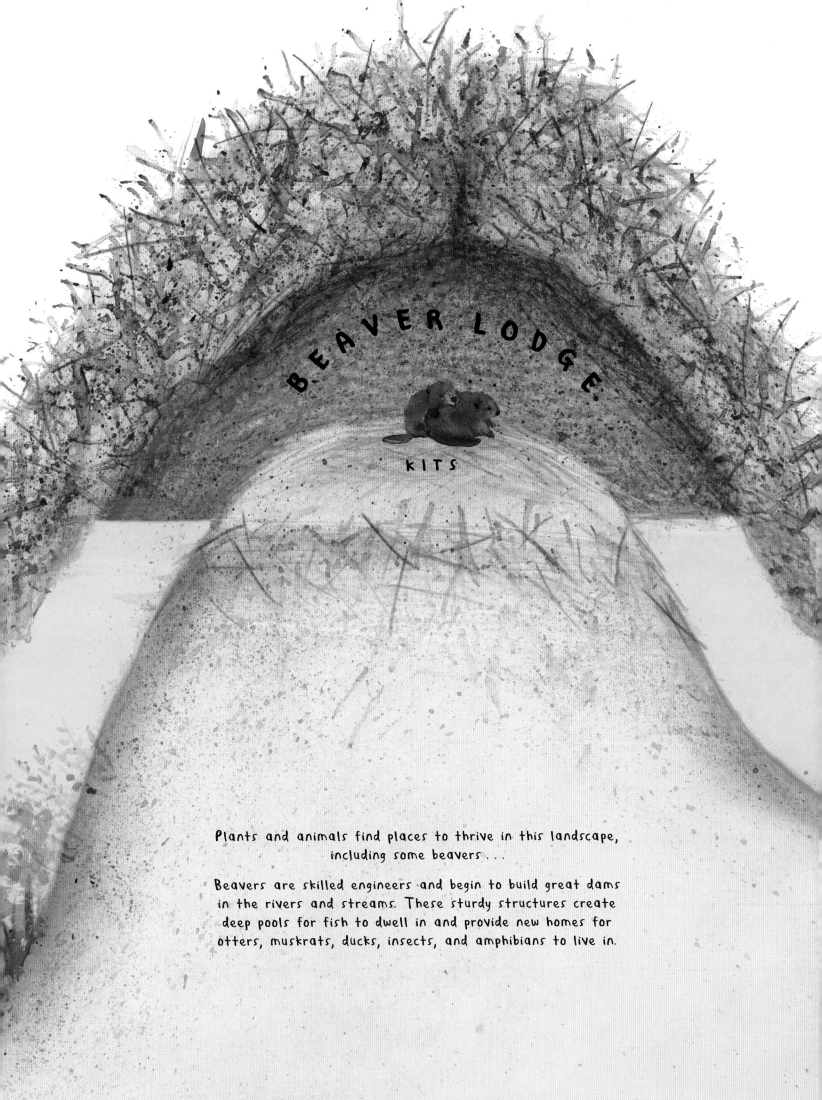

BEAVER LODGE

KITS

Plants and animals find places to thrive in this landscape,
including some beavers . . .

Beavers are skilled engineers and begin to build great dams
in the rivers and streams. These sturdy structures create
deep pools for fish to dwell in and provide new homes for
otters, muskrats, ducks, insects, and amphibians to live in.

BEETLES
AND BEARS

Once the wolf packs have eaten
their fill, they leave carcasses that
other animals can scavenge.

Beetles and other insects thrive on these abandoned kills.

But creepy-crawlies are not the only ones who enjoy the
scraps—the bears come to tuck in too. With more meat
to eat, the number of bears in Yellowstone grows. They
soon become a match for the wolves, challenging them
for food and slumping over carcasses to claim them
as their own.

Scavengers from the air also race to join in
the feast. Ravens, magpies, and eagles
trail the wolves as they hunt,
snatching their share.

THE LANDSCAPE CHANGES

From high in the sky, the eagle
sees what no one else yet can.

The shapes of the rivers begin to flow in straighter
paths ... Anchored by the roots of new trees, the
riverbanks strengthen and so they collapse less often.
Eventually the rivers narrow and pools form—
perfect spaces for fish to splash and swim.

From still waters to dappled shade, open plains to
deep forests, blue skies to ecosystems far underwater,
Yellowstone National Park is being restored.

Scientists are still discovering
the role of the wolf in this
ever-changing wilderness.

THE RETURN OF THE WOLF

In 1995, fourteen wolves were reintroduced to Yellowstone. They threaded their way across the valleys, leaving behind the first new wolf tracks in nearly seventy years.

In total, forty-one wolves were brought to Yellowstone over two years. They are the ancestors of about ten packs of wolves that howl and hunt in the park today.

Today, Yellowstone is as wild as ever. But in summer its roads are busy. Tourists come to see its spectacular hot-water fountains and watch wildlife splashing in the alpine rivers, beavers building magnificent dams, and bison nibbling their way across wide, lush valleys. With patience and sharp eyes, those who are lucky may spot a wolf.

The wolves stay back, away from the crowds. On the hunt . . . On the move . . . Wolves following food.

FOURTEEN WOLVES

The wolves that were released into Yellowstone
National Park in 1995 were fitted with tracking devices.
This is how their lives unfolded.

Wolf 1

The first wolf caught in Canada
was tagged incorrectly and released
into Idaho. The wolves that were
successfully released into Yellowstone
were numbered 2 to 15.

Wolf 4

Crystal Creek Pack

Alpha male

Died in conflict with
Druid Pack, 1996

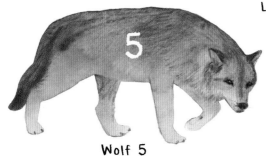

Wolf 2

Crystal Creek Pack / Leopold Pack

Male

Mated with Wolf 7 to form
Leopold Pack

Killed by other wolves, 2002

Wolf 3

Crystal Creek Pack

Male

Left pack to live independently

Shot by Animal Damage
Control for repeatedly
harassing sheep, 1996

Wolf 6

Crystal Creek Pack

Male

Killed by a bull elk, 1998

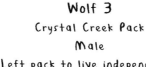

Wolf 5

Crystal Creek Pack

Alpha female

Established a new territory after
the death of Wolf 4

Disappeared 2002, date of death unknown

Rose Creek Pack / Leopold Pack
Female
Mated with Wolf 2 to form
Leopold Pack
Killed by other wolves, 2002

Crystal Creek Pack / Rose Creek Pack
Male
Left Crystal Creek Pack to mate with
Wolf 9 in Rose Creek Pack
Died naturally, 2000

Rose Creek Pack
Female
Her original mate (Wolf 10)
was poached, so mated
with Wolf 8
Disappeared, presumed dead
2002

Soda Butte Pack
Female
Illegally shot, 1996

Rose Creek Pack
Male
Illegally shot, 1995

Soda Butte Pack
Male
Separated from the pack
Illegally shot, 1996

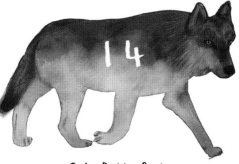

Soda Butte Pack
Female
Mated with Wolf 13
Died in a battle with a
bull moose, 2000

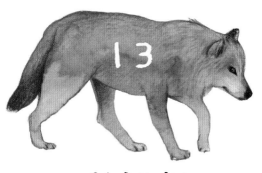

Soda Butte Pack
Male
Mated with Wolf 14
Nicknamed "Old Blue"
Died of old age, 1997

Soda Butte Pack
Male
Shot for damaging
livestock, 1997

· PART THREE ·

UNDERSTANDING HOW NATURE WORKS

In nature, animals and plants depend on each other to survive.

It is like a jigsaw puzzle, where everything fits together to create a big picture. In nature, this big, complicated picture is the ecosystem.

When a top predator disappears or reappears, it changes the balance of a whole ecosystem, affecting even the smallest forms of life. This top-down domino effect is called a **TROPHIC CASCADE.**

The balance of nature in Yellowstone depends on the seasonal movement of elk in and out of the park's borders, the harshness of winter, the threat of hunters beyond the park's borders, and the rise and fall of other predators. This trophic cascade is an evolving story.

Small predators

Coyotes tried to take the wolves' place at the top of the food chain. Their numbers started to climb and they became more powerful in the park, but they couldn't control the growing numbers of elk.

COYOTES

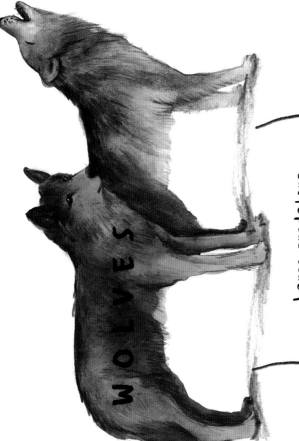

WOLVES

Large predators

Wolves hunt large herbivores, such as elk. Their presence in the park keeps elk numbers down. It also forces the elk to stay on the move, which prevents them from overgrazing the same patch of land.

Elk

When there were no wolves to hunt them, elk numbers increased. They overpopulated the park. These huge herds had enormous appetites, and so they ate the new tree saplings and grazed the land.

ELK

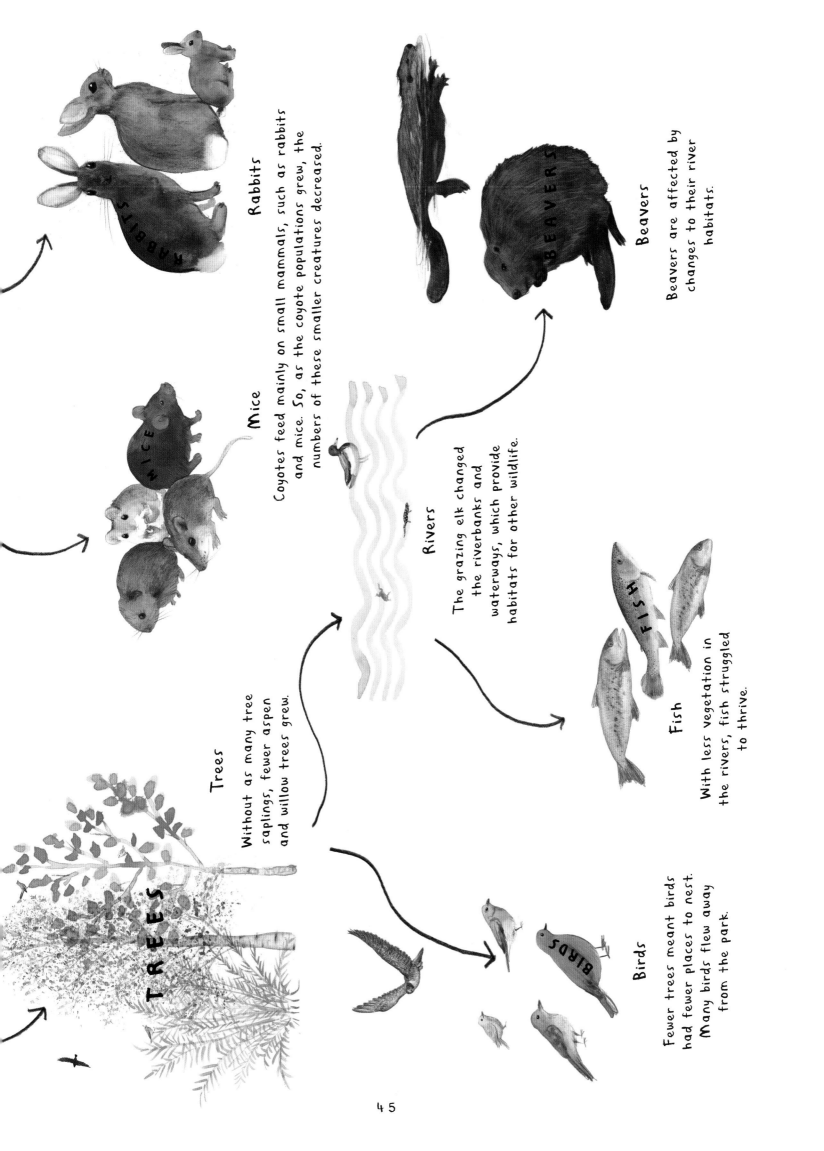

Rabbits

Coyotes feed mainly on small mammals, such as rabbits and mice. So, as the coyote populations grew, the numbers of these smaller creatures decreased.

Mice

Beavers

Beavers are affected by changes to their river habitats.

Rivers

The grazing elk changed the riverbanks and waterways, which provide habitats for other wildlife.

Trees

Without as many tree saplings, fewer aspen and willow trees grew.

Fish

With less vegetation in the rivers, fish struggled to thrive.

Birds

Fewer trees meant birds had fewer places to nest. Many birds flew away from the park.

REWILDING AND CONSERVATION

Rewilding allows nature to take control, restoring a healthy environment for wildlife and people.

This can restore land that has been damaged by bringing plants and animals back to places where they once thrived. Often these projects bring back keystone species—species that help hold a whole habitat together—whose absence has altered the lives of the other animals that live there. The return of wolves to Yellowstone National Park is a world-famous example of rewilding.

Rewilding is different from conservation. In a conservation project, people plan to help protect an individual species or habitat with a particular result in mind. For example, conservation projects might involve people planting trees to restore a forest, whereas in a rewilding project trees are left to seed themselves, so nature decides what happens next.
Both are important in restoring biodiversity to our natural world.

There are many projects all over the world where animal species are reintroduced to benefit the natural world.

United Kingdom

The native UK beaver was hunted to extinction in the sixteenth century for its fur and meat. Without beavers' brilliant canal- and dam-building skills, the water in rivers became polluted and many flooded. Beavers are being reintroduced from Scotland in some places. These wildlife engineers help protect land from flooding and create wetland habitats for all kinds of river life.

BEAVER

South Korea

With their elegant fur, tigers are one of the world's most poached animals and so are now an endangered species. Without tigers, large herbivores are multiplying and eating away the vegetation. The tiger forest in South Korea has created a large, safe space for tigers to breed. Males and females are reared in captivity before being released into the wild.
The tigers' return has begun to restore the balance between plant and animal life.

AMUR TIGER

Netherlands

Bison were hunted to near extinction in Europe at the beginning of the twentieth century. In 2007, they were brought back to the Netherlands to help with something that was becoming a big problem—grass! There was so much grass that it was limiting plant biodiversity. To restore the land, something needed to come in and eat a lot of the grass. And bison have a huge appetite!

Galapagos Islands

In 2010, scientists estimated that, despite being one of the most famous native Galapagos species, only 10 percent of giant tortoises were left in the wild. Today, scientists collect these endangered tortoises' eggs and raise the babies in captivity. The tortoises are put back into the wild once they are strong enough to protect themselves. Now, giant tortoise numbers are increasing. The tortoises have also helped new trees to grow by spreading their seeds in their poop as they plod around.

Philippines

As these giants move through the water, they churn the ocean's nutrients. Whale poop also feeds lots of very small species, such as krill, plankton, and even algae, which other marine life, such as dolphins and fish, like to feed on. These tiny species absorb excess carbon from the air and water, which helps to keep the CO_2 levels in our climate stable. However, whale numbers have drastically decreased due to commercial whaling, entanglement in fishing nets, and warming waters changing their habitat. Many whales are found stranded on beaches. In the Philippines, scientists and wildlife charities are training people to rescue stranded whales and help them get home, where they keep the ocean ecosystem moving.

WHY PREDATORS MATTER

Rewilding is hugely important for restoring wild species on land and in seas.

However, there is sometimes conflict between people and wildlife. Wolf wars still rage. Luckily, in Yellowstone National Park, wolves are safe because there are laws that protect them. But wolves don't read maps and so they often wander beyond the park's borders, where they may meet hunters' deadly guns.

Although they were once feared, the wolves of Yellowstone have shown the world why predators matter. They support all life because they help keep nature in balance and the ecosystem stable.

Around the globe, people are finding ways to share space with keystone species such as wolves, because humans too depend on a healthy natural world to survive.